Tyrannosaurus rex

Tyrannosaurus rex

Heather Amery

Illustrated by Tony Gibbons

DINOSAUR COLLECTION

PARRAGON

Contents

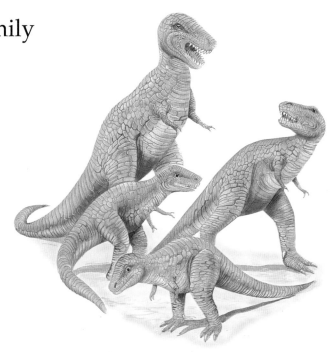

Introducing
Tyrannosaurus rex

Enormous and terrifying, **Tyrannosaurus rex** (TIE-<u>RAN</u>-OH-<u>SAW</u>-RUS <u>RECKS</u>), was a monster – the fiercest dinosaur of all time.

It ate other dinosaurs, biting them with huge teeth and ripping their flesh with long claws. Other dinosaurs were terrified of it.

They would run away if they saw **Tyrannosaurus** coming.

How long ago did **Tyrannosaurus rex** live? What was its favourite meal? And where did it live?

Read on, and find out all about this meat-eating creature that once ruled the Earth!

5

The changing planet

Scientists believe that the Earth is about 4,600 million years old. At first, it was just a huge ball of boiling hot rocks and metals. Slowly, the surface cooled and hardened into a crust. This cracked into several giant pieces which moved very slowly apart over many millions of years. Eventually, these pieces became the land and the sea-bed. The rains then came to make the seas.

To begin with, the land was one big continent, with sea all around it. Later, it began to split.

This was in the **Triassic Period (1)**, 225 million years ago, when the first dinosaurs lived. About 50 million years later, in the **Jurassic Period (2)**, the land began to break up further. Many new types of dinosaur now appeared.

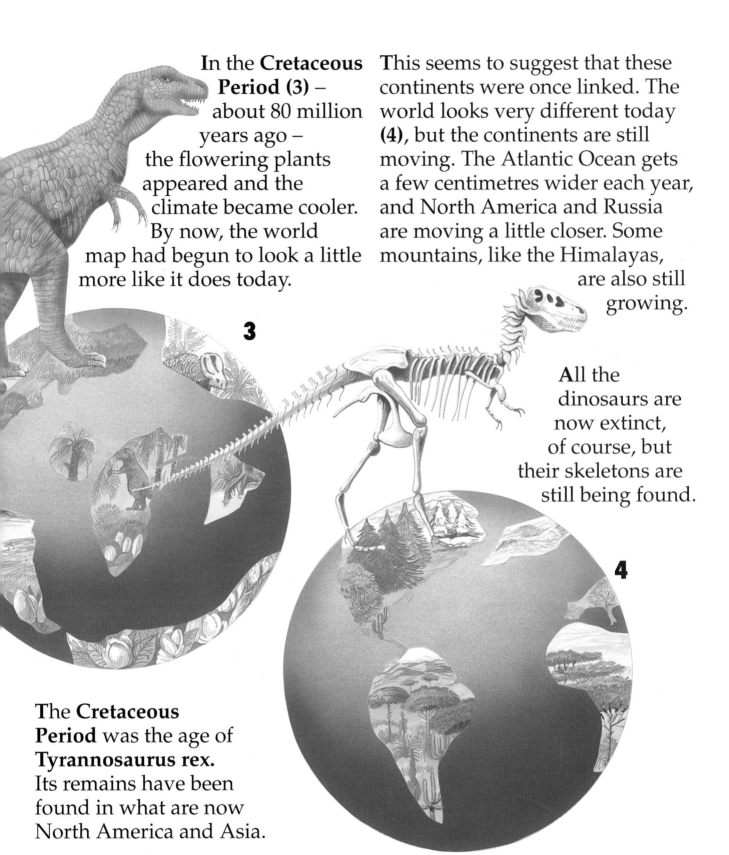

In the **Cretaceous Period (3)** – about 80 million years ago – the flowering plants appeared and the climate became cooler. By now, the world map had begun to look a little more like it does today.

This seems to suggest that these continents were once linked. The world looks very different today **(4)**, but the continents are still moving. The Atlantic Ocean gets a few centimetres wider each year, and North America and Russia are moving a little closer. Some mountains, like the Himalayas, are also still growing.

All the dinosaurs are now extinct, of course, but their skeletons are still being found.

3

4

The **Cretaceous Period** was the age of **Tyrannosaurus rex.** Its remains have been found in what are now North America and Asia.

Giant discovery

8

The first fairly good skeleton of a **Tyrannosaurus rex** was dug up in 1902, in Montana, in the United States of America.

It included parts of the skull and jaws, as well as bits of the backbone, shoulder, hips and legs. This skeleton was taken to the American Museum of Natural History in New York.

Before this time, many huge teeth and odd bones had been discovered. But no one knew to which dinosaur they belonged.

The dinosaur bones were looked at by a famous fossil-hunter called Henry Fairfield Osborn. He was the first to identify **Tyrannosaurus rex** and gave it this name, which means 'king of the tyrant reptiles'.

Tyrannosaurus rex was probably the fiercest meat-eating dinosaur ever to have lived on the Earth. It was also one of the biggest – as long as two buses, as tall as a giraffe and as heavy as an elephant. You might only have reached up to its knee!

It had a huge head and could open its jaws so wide that it could have swallowed a man whole. Luckily, there were no humans around at the time.

In 1990, palaeontologists – the name given to scientists who study prehistoric remains – dug up the world's largest skeleton of **Tyrannosaurus rex** in South Dakota, USA.

But the palaeontologists found this skeleton, which they nicknamed Sue, on land that belongs to the Sioux Indians. Today, palaeontologists and Indians are still arguing over who owns the skeleton.

Millions of years ago

About 67 million years ago, in the Cretaceous Period when **Tyrannosaurus rex** lived, the Earth looked very different from the way it does today. The weather was much cooler than it had been, but there were no very cold winters – even in the far north.

Herds of dinosaurs wandered in the forests, looking for food. The first flowering plants grew at this time. There was no grass as yet. But plant-eating dinosaurs, such as **Euplocephalus** (YOO-PLO-SEFF-A-LUS), with its small teeth and weak jaws, grazed on ground ferns. With other dinosaurs, it nibbled on the first oak and magnolia trees, which often grew near streams.

Crocodiles, turtles and fish swam in the shallow rivers, while long-necked reptiles, known as plesiosaurs, swam in the seas.

In the salty river mouths, there were giant lizards, called mosasaurs. These grew up to 10m – that's as long as a bus.

Dragonflies and other flying insects buzzed in the air. Beetles, crickets and cockroaches crawled among the mosses, and snakes slithered through the ferns. Up above, in the skies, flew great bat-like reptiles called pterosaurs.

The very large plant-eating dinosaurs – such as **Brachiosaurus** (<u>BRAK</u>-EE-OH-<u>SAW</u>-RUS) – had mostly died out by now, but smaller ones still roamed the land. Giant meat-eaters, such as **Tyrannosaurus rex**, hunted and ate them.

Some of the smaller dinosaurs had armoured bodies, and even tail-clubs with which to ward off attackers who thought they would make a good meal. But if **Tyrannosaurus** was hungry and caught them, they would have found it very difficult to defend themselves against its mighty jaws.

11

Monster bones

Tyrannosaurus rex was a huge, heavy dinosaur with an enormous skeleton. It walked on massive back legs, holding up its long tail to balance itself.

Its back feet were very large. One foot was more than six times as big as yours. Each back foot had four toes, three facing forwards and one backwards, with sharp, curved claws.

The backward-facing toe did not touch the ground. The bones in its feet were locked together to give it extra strength.

At the end of its very small front legs, there were two long claws as well. But they were too far from **Tyrannosaurus'** mouth for them to be used for feeding. Some scientists think that **Tyrannosaurus** held on to its enemies with its claws, and that it used its front legs to push itself up off the ground after it had been resting.

Its neck was thick with very strong muscles. This meant that it could twist

and turn its head when tearing at its food.

Tyrannosaurus rex tore at its prey with teeth which were extremely sharp. It gobbled up any dead dinosaurs that it found and also killed plant-eating dinosaurs which were too slow, old or ill to run away. It probably ate its own weight in meat every few days.

Tyrannosaurus rex's skull was very large and strong. With its powerful jaw muscles, it could take giant bites using its enormous teeth and could eat great chunks of meat without even chewing. It could have swallowed you in one mouthful!

Some dinosaurs may have had eyes at the side of their heads. But scientists think that **Tyrannosaurus rex** had eyes that faced forwards, helping it to focus on its prey when it was out for the kill.

Although it was so big, **Tyrannosaurus rex** had

very powerful legs and may have been able to run quite fast over short distances. A charging **Tyrannosaurus** must have been one of the most terrifying sights on Earth!

Most terrifying of all must have been a battle between two adult **Tyrannosaurus rex** over food.

Dinosaur attack!

Tyrannosaurus rex prowled about, scavenging for dead dinosaurs to eat and seeking out any tasty-looking live dinosaurs it could kill.

But some of the smaller, plant-eating dinosaurs could put up a good fight against **Tyrannosaurus.**

If a **Triceratops** (TRY-<u>SER</u>-A-TOPS) was threatened, for example, it could defend itself with its sharp horns. Others in the herd may also have come to the rescue by charging the enemy.

So **Tyrannosaurus** may soon have realized that its next meal was not going to be a **Triceratops.** Not only that, if **Tyrannosaurus** did not get away quickly enough, it might be wounded.

Fearful predator

It was a warm afternoon, about 70 million years ago. A hungry **Tyrannosaurus rex** plodded through the

Which poor creature would it have for lunch?

trees and ferns, looking for a meal. Turning its great head from side to side, it snapped its enormous jaws.

Tyrannosaurus had not eaten for some time, and was in a bad mood.

Ahead, it had caught sight of a lone **Parasaurolophus** (PAR-A-SAUR-OH-LOAF-US), quietly browsing on clumps of low bushes. **Tyrannosaurus** crept up to it quietly, taking care not to let the smaller dinosaur know it was there.

16

Suddenly, **Tyrannosaurus rex** charged at its unlucky victim. The giant meat-eater's feet thundered on the ground as it ran. **Parasaurolophus** looked quickly round, sensing danger.

Tyrannosaurus tore at the creature's back with sharp claws. **Parasaurolophus** screamed with fear and pain, then crashed to the ground, struggling to escape. But the battle was soon over.

After an hour or two, the victor had eaten its fill and there was

It gave one strange hoot of alarm and started to dash away.

But it was too late. **Tyrannosaurus** pounced, sinking its huge teeth into **Parasaurolophus'** neck. As it did so, it gave out a terrifying roar.

little left of **Parasaurolophus** – just its bones. **Tyrannosaurus** now lumbered away to sleep off its heavy meal.

The Tyrannosaurid family

Tyrannosaurus rex was one member of a group, or family, of dinosaurs called **Tyrannosaurids**. Scientists think they were the biggest meat-eating animals which have ever lived on land.

All the members of this family had huge heads with big teeth, very large bodies, powerful back legs and long claws. Most of them lived about 90 – 65 million years ago, in the Cretaceous Period.

Albertosaurus, (AL-<u>BERT</u>-OH-<u>SAW</u>-RUS) **(1)**, looked a lot like **Tyrannosaurus rex**, but as you can see it was rather smaller.

Its name means 'Alberta lizard', since its bones were first found in Alberta, Canada.

Tarbosaurus, (<u>TAR</u>-BO-<u>SAW</u>-RUS) **(2)**, – whose name means 'alarming lizard' – was another huge relative. It was nearly as big as **Tyrannosaurus,** but less heavy.

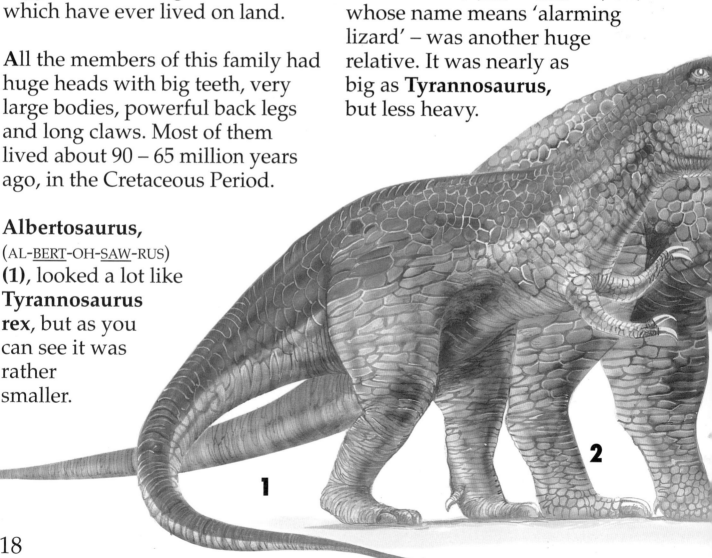

1

2

Its skull was longer than **Tyrannosaurus',** and had 27 large, knife-like teeth in the upper jaw. These would have sliced easily through any victim's flesh. **Tarbosaurus'** remains have been found in Mongolia, Asia.

Tyrannosaurus rex (3) was the biggest and heaviest member of the **Tyrannosaurid** family.

Daspletosaurus, (DA-SPLEET-OH-SAW-RUS) **(4),** looked like its cousins and has a name that means 'frightful lizard'.

3

4

19

Tyrannosaurus data

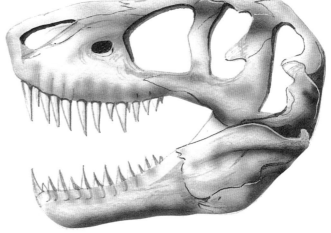

Tyrannosaurus rex was one of the fiercest, largest and most powerful meat-eating dinosaurs that ever lived. It roamed the plains of North America and China, charging at herds of harmless plant-eating dinosaurs, killing them and then feeding on their bodies.

Terrifying teeth

The tooth shown here is not even as big as one of **Tyrannosaurus rex's** teeth. It had two rows of sharp teeth, shaped like this. The sides of each tooth had a jagged edge, like a steak knife, which it used to tear at its meat. Scientists believe that if a tooth broke off in a fight, a new one soon grew in its place.

Huge skull

A **Tyrannosaurus rex** skull was over a metre long and had powerful muscles for biting meat and crunching up bones. There were holes in the bones of the skull to make it lighter.

Sharp claws

On its back feet, there were sharp claws, used to attack and rip apart other dinosaurs. **Tyrannosaurus** had three toes which pointed forward and one smaller toe which pointed backwards.

20

Terrible roar

Lumbering along in search of food, **Tyrannosaurus rex** must have let out terrifying roars that frightened other dinosaurs. By roaring, it could also have kept in touch with the members of its family.

Fast runner

Although **Tyrannosaurus rex** was so big and heavy, it could run quite fast on its sturdy back legs when chasing other dinosaurs. Scientists can tell this from its long ankle bones.

Family packs

Families of **Tyrannosaurus rex** probably lived together in a herd until the young ones were old enough to find and kill their own food.

End of the dinosaurs

About 65 million years ago, all the dinosaurs suddenly died out. No one really knows why, but there are plenty of ideas.

One theory is that a meteorite, a giant chunk of rock from outer space, hit the Earth. It caused such thick clouds of dust and steam that the Sun was blotted out for weeks or even months. Without sunlight, plants could not grow and the dinosaurs may have starved to death.

Some scientists say, however, that the sea-levels rose and flooded the land where many dinosaurs lived. This theory is backed up by the fact that many types of sea creature became extinct with the dinosaurs.

According to another theory, a star exploded in the sky, showering the Earth with deadly rays. But if this is true, how did lots of other animals and birds survive?

Whatever it was that caused the death of the dinosaurs, for some mysterious reason smaller animals managed to survive.

First published 1993
by Parragon Book Service, Bristol

Text and illustrations copyright
© 1993 Quartz Editorial Services
112 Station Road, Edgware HA8 7AQ

ISBN 1–85813–318–1

Printed and bound in Great Britain by BPCC Paulton Books